STAY GRATEFUL

A guide to help kids and the adults in their lives practice gratitude

Written by Salpi Dunlap

Illustrated by London and Lincoln Dunlap

Stay Grateful
Copyright Text © 2019 Salpi Dunlap
Copyright Illustrations © 2019 London and Lincoln Dunlap
Edited by Michael Molenda

Second Edition printed in 2022

All rights reserved. No part of this publication may be reproduced or transmitted in any form or by any means, mechanical or electronic, including photocopying, recording, or otherwise, or stored in a retrieval system, without prior permission from the publisher.

For more information, contact:
Salpi Dunlap at
salpi@staytruebooks.com
www.staytruebooks.com

ISBN 978-0-578-58981-7

DEDICATION

This book is dedicated to my friends and family. Thank you for your support.

FOREWORD

I found myself crying in the bathroom a few years back. I was upset with where I thought my life was going, but at that moment, I had one of those ah-ha moments. Earlier, I had come across an article about practicing gratitude, and I thought, "It can't be this easy." Well, I'm here to tell you that it is.

Practicing gratitude changed my life. I was surprised to discover that it's not the *thing* that makes you happy—it's the feeling inside of you that is awakened. This power is already inside you. You only need to change your perception—the way you see and think about things.

For example, my kids and I each have our own gratitude journals. In the morning, we write about what we are grateful for, and what our hopes are for the day. At night, we write about our favorite part of the day and how we could have made that day even better.

I write these books for kids, but my hope is to pass along the message to adults, as well. The sooner we start practicing gratitude, the sooner our lives will change for the better. Let's start today!

ACKNOWLEDGEMENTS

I would like to take this opportunity to thank my family and friends for all of their support during my delve into gratitude and self-discovery.

BREATHING

Before you start reading this book, take a minute to practice your breathing. Sit in a comfortable position and close your eyes. Take a deep breath in while counting to four. Hold it in for one second and slowly breathe out, counting to five. Do this six more times.

Feel your body relax with every exhale. Relax your face, your neck, your shoulders, your arms, your tummy, and your legs. Every time you breathe out, feel your muscles relax even more.

Now you're ready to open your eyes and start reading!

DISCOVERING

The source of gratitude already exists inside of you. You don't need to search for it outside of yourself—it is in your heart. By changing your perception, you can live a grateful life.

For example, two people are washing their cars. One is thinking about all the bad things in his life. He is upset, sweaty, thirsty, and not having any fun. The other person is focusing on the good things in her life. She is sweaty and thirsty, too, but she is grateful for the sunshine and having a car to drive. These people are performing the same tasks, but they are having different perceptions. Always remember you have a choice on how you view your surroundings.

Try to change your perceptions to celebrate the good, by making a list of ten things you're grateful for each day. Start with things you may not actively think about, such as food, shelter, your health, and anything else you take for granted. Keep this list where you will see it every day.

TRANSFORMING

Gratitude brings transformation. Whenever you are grateful for something, you are creating new pathways in your brain that are changing your perceptions—such as being aware of all the good things in your life.

Practice being grateful. When you feel happy, think about the *reason* you are happy. Then say, "Thank you for this moment." And remember this feeling.

The more you practice this, the better you will get at finding reasons to be grateful. Gratitude can be your flashlight when your mind is lost in the dark, or sad, or upset. For example, if you find yourself feeling down, come up with three things you are grateful for in that moment. Allow your awareness to expand and find the good in times of strife.

Turning gratitude into a daily practice will transform you so much that you will barely recognize who you were in the past. You will feel like a different person, and you will react to things with more patience and love.

FEELING

How do you feel inside when you feel thankful towards someone? Do you smile? Does your heart fill with joy? Allow yourself to feel that emotion in your mind and in your body. Then, imagine that person accepting your gratitude. The more grateful you are, the more things you will find to be grateful for.

Experiencing these emotions will remind you of being grateful. When you are feeling negative emotions such as anger or stress, your heart will feel closed. A closed heart cannot feel gratitude. Instead, focus on the joyful things in your life. The next time you are sad or upset, remember to think of something positive.

Set up reminders around your house, your room, or your desk at school. These are just little notes to yourself. All it takes is a piece of paper and a message. Write "I choose to focus on the positive," or "I am thankful for _____ today," or "I'm so lucky to have _____ in my life." There are lots of ways to think about gratitude.

MEDITATING

In the first book of this series, *Stay True*, we talked about meditating to stay present. Meditation also allows us to stay grateful, because it can give our brains a rest when we are feeling overwhelmed. We use our brains for so much stuff, and sometimes it just needs a break!

When your brain is at rest, it can relax and help you focus on what really matters. Start by meditating for one minute at a time, and then increase the time as you get more comfortable with it. Sit still and focus on your breathing. Slowly breathe in and out, thinking only about your breath and no other thoughts. This can be difficult at first, but with practice you will get better. The more you meditate, the calmer your brain will feel over time.

NOTICING

The more grateful you are, the more you notice the joy and beauty that surrounds you—which, in turn, allows you to be even more grateful!

Gratitude is a cycle that flows through your thoughts and brings you peace. The key is to practice until gratitude becomes a daily habit. A daily habit can become a lifestyle, and once gratitude becomes a lifestyle, you will have uncovered the secret to finding happiness in every moment.

Even the most boring things—such as cleaning your room—won't seem as bad anymore. In fact, say this the next time you are making your bed: "Thank you for this bed." When you are folding or hanging up your clothes, say, "Thank you for these clothes." When you're putting your toys away, say, "Thank you for these toys." You will start to realize how much love and gratitude you have in your heart. And when your heart is filled with love and gratitude, there is no room left for negative thoughts.

PRACTICING

Living a life of gratitude means opening our eyes to the beauty that surrounds us. An easy place to practice gratitude is in nature. Go on a hike and explore your surroundings. Take the time to notice the trees, the leaves, the flowers, and the clouds in the sky. What do you smell? What do you hear? When you connect with nature, it's easy to be grateful for it.

Practicing gratitude will help you awaken your true self. Your worries and anxieties will become smaller, and your joy and compassion will continue to grow.

MISTAKING

We all make mistakes. When we have a hard time with something, we tend to focus on the negative.

For example, when my son Lincoln took a spelling test at school, he realized he had made a mistake on one of the words when he got home. He was very upset about that one word, instead of focusing on the words he had spelled correctly. We took a minute to practice our breathing, and we repeated: "It's okay to make mistakes. I don't have to be perfect."

After a few minutes, Lincoln was able to be grateful about the words he spelled correctly. It was difficult at first, but he realized he could choose his reaction. We all do.

Instead of reacting to an obstacle negatively, embrace it as an opportunity to meet a challenge with gratitude. There's a gift in every moment, and you get to choose how you accept it and respond to it.

SHIFTING

We just talked about how life is not perfect, and that we all make mistakes. When we feel empty, jealous, sad, or angry, we want to fill that void—that feeling of emptiness and despair. Practicing gratitude helps us see that we can be complete, just as we are.

Gratitude helps us learn how to appreciate what we have in this moment. It shifts our perspective to the present, and how can change our life for the better.

When you say "thank you" to the present moment, you are learning to be grateful for the things in your life right now. You are not thinking about the future, or how you wish things were different. You are saying "yes" to your life as it is. This helps you feel complete, and when you are complete, you no longer feel the need to fill an emptiness inside.

HEALING

Gratitude brings healing. We learned in *Stay True*, that we have choices we can make every day. You can choose to be grateful, and practicing gratefulness not only helps your mind, it also keeps your body healthy. You will find you are less sad, anxious, and stressed.

You *can* train your brain to change. When the brain receives positive or negative input, it reacts to it accordingly. Choose to fill your mind with powerful positive input—such as gratitude—which makes our brains and bodies feel better.

Start your day by thinking positive thoughts. And when you experience joy, remember to say, "Thank you for this moment." Even when things don't go your way, or something happens that makes you sad, remember to think about something you are grateful for, and notice the shift in your heart and your mind. If you allow it, you will feel joy enter your heart, even in the most difficult times. When our hearts feel good, we begin to heal from the inside.

APPRECIATING

Let's appreciate even the simplest things in our lives. For me, the simple things I'm grateful for are food, water, a roof over my head, and clothes and shoes to wear. Then, I start to think about how comfortable my bed is, and how lucky we are to have music and art in our lives. When I see the sun for the first time in the morning, I say, "Good morning, sun. Thank you for being here."

Make a list of the things you appreciate. Your list may stay the same or it may change every day. Use this list as a reminder if your thoughts get lost in everyday stress. Practicing gratitude will bring your heart the same joy you feel when you see something that makes you happy.

LOVING

"She loved life, and it loved her right back."

These words—from Kobi Yamada's poem, *She*—are what I live by every day. An easy way to learn to love your life is to be grateful for the little things. Those little things can add up to big things, and before you know it, you will have found the recipe for living your own happy life!

When your heart is filled with love, you feel good. Did you know you have infinite love in your heart? You have enough for yourself, and enough to give away to others. When someone is sad, try cheering them up by saying something like, "I care about you." Kind words are always a good way to spread love and gratitude.

When you come from a place of love, you cannot fail.

EXPRESSING

Gratitude is an expression of love. Love is activated when it is expressed, and one way to express love is to *tell* your family and friends how much you care about them. Love can also be shown by your actions. You can *show* love by not necessarily saying it.

But first, express gratitude for yourself. Think of two things you love about yourself, and say, "Thank you" for them.

Now, take a moment to think about how you can express love to someone in your life. Think of how *you* would feel if someone told you how happy they are that you're in their life.

On the other hand, if you have *negative* feelings towards someone, find reasons to be grateful for them. The negative feelings will start to disappear, and you will feel closer to that person. When you express your gratitude to them, there will be an exchange of healing energy between you. You will instantly feel more connected to them.

CONNECTING

Gratitude allows us to connect with our true selves by connecting with what truly matters in our lives. Deeply appreciating what we already have will attract more abundance to our lives. This is because connecting with our true selves also builds confidence. When we are confident, we believe we are worthy of attracting good things.

Anything is possible when we've made this connection.

Now, this may sound a bit silly, but it's important. Say, "I'm grateful for my gratitude." Honor your hard work, and how far you've come. Empower yourself to continue what you've accomplished so far.

TRUSTING

Trusting the process of practicing gratitude makes it easier to accept it into your life. If you trust gratitude as a solution to your problems, it will work much quicker.

One day, Lincoln got in the car to go home from school, and I could tell he was in a bad mood. He said, "My whole entire day was terrible." After we talked about it, I said, "I'm sure if you try really hard, you can find something positive about your day." But he stayed upset.

After some breathing exercises, he came around and thought of one thing that was good in his day. I helped him focus on that, and soon, he forgot about his bad day.

With more practice, Lincoln will realize he can trust gratitude to turn his moods around. He'll remember that thinking about something positive helped him feel better—instead of letting the negative thoughts keep him in a bad mood all day. Realizing he has the power to choose positivity, will build trust in gratitude.

GROWING

It's easy to feel grateful when you're happy. It's *not* so easy when you're upset. Happily, when you develop a personal healing practice to improve the quality of your life, you have accomplished inner growth—the mindfulness to integrate emotions, thoughts, and experiences in the moment to help you deal with new negative experiences.

Gratitude doesn't make negative things disappear—it helps you find a healthy way to deal with them. Once you are prepared to deal with negative experiences, you'll get through them much faster.

LIVING

You are now ready to live every day in gratitude!

In this book, we have talked about practicing gratitude every day until it becomes a habit. When gratitude becomes a natural way of life, you won't need to remember how to be grateful. Those thankful thoughts will already be in your brain. Gratitude becomes the natural way to express who you are and how you feel.

Gratitude brings freedom from negative thoughts, and it helps you stay true to yourself—to be authentic. You are responsible for your own life stories. Take charge of *your* story. Don't blame others when things don't go your way. By taking control, you can also take credit for the joys and blessings in your life, and you'll realize you deserve it.

When you are in a state of gratefulness, the Universe will sense that you are connected to your true self, and it will help you stay in that state. The Universe wants you to be happy and to succeed.

Gratitude helps you feel supported and abundant.

MANTRAS

Mantras are personal affirmations meant to motivate and encourage. Here is a list of mantras that were used in this book:

Thank you for this moment.
I am so grateful for this moment.
I choose to focus on the positive.
When I think about _____, it makes me happy.
I am thankful for _____ today.
I'm so lucky to have _____ in my life.
Thank you for this bed.
Thank you for these clothes.
Thank you for these toys.
It's okay to make mistakes.
I don't have to be perfect.
I am grateful for myself.
I am grateful to be here on this planet at this time.
I'm grateful for my gratitude.

ABOUT THE AUTHOR

Salpi is the mother of three beautiful children. She started on her spiritual journey years ago but didn't realize it until 2016. Since then, she has practiced gratitude and living in the moment—which changed her perspective on happiness. Her quality of life has greatly improved, and all she did was change the way she looks at things!

Her intent is to share this message with people of all ages. It's never too early or too late to start staying true.

Her two youngest children, London and Lincoln, are the illustrators of this book. Salpi wrote the words, and then asked them to draw whatever came to mind to portray the words on the page.

The result was pure magic.

www.ingramcontent.com/pod-product-compliance
Lightning Source LLC
Chambersburg PA
CBHW061403090426
42743CB00003B/124